Forgiven

Healing the wounds of

ABORTION

with

CHRIST

TABITHA LAVENDER

Cover & Interior Design by Kendra Cagle, www.5LakesDesign.com

ISBN-10: 978-1-946208-95-8

Dedication

This book is dedicated to Stephen, Nicole, and Alexander, and women all over the world who have had abortions and long to be set free from all the darkness connected to abortion.

He heals the brokenhearted
And binds up their wounds [healing their
pain and comforting their sorrow].

—Psalm 147:3 (Amplified)

Contents

Introduction

—WHY BREAK THE SILENCE

There were four of us—all women—sitting in our Bible study leader's living room. It was right before the study was going to start that one lady began to talk about how when she was a teenager, her mother made her have an abortion. That opened the floodgate—and the rest of us began to chime in.

"I had an abortion too when I was a teenager," another one of us admitted.

I spoke, "I had an abortion. I've actually had more than one. It's not something I normally tell people."

Of the four of us, all but one had not had an abortion. Three out of four, 75%, of the women in that room, all of whom had become followers of Christ, had had abortions . . .

Next we talked about our reasons:

"I was only 13 years old, and I knew I could not take care of a baby. And there was no way that my mother was going to allow me to have a baby. It would have looked terrible for her. She had an image to uphold."

"The boy I was messing around with was an arrogant punk. There is no way that he would have been a good father, and he would have been in my life much longer than I would have liked."

"I had a future career to think about. I wanted to finish college, and a baby did not fit into that plan. And I did not want to have a baby and not be married to the father."

Faith, the Bible study leader, listening to our conversation, suggested that some of our reasons were more legitimate than others—and that split the room. I fell into a shameful silence. The other two sat up straighter, feeling justified and righteous.

Shortly thereafter, the remaining members arrived, and we began the Bible study. After that time, we never talked about abortion again. We seemed to go on with our lives.

There are many women, both in the body of Christ and not in the body of Christ, that have had abortions. According to an article published on the Guttmacher Policy Review website, three in 10 women will have had an abortion by the age of 45. Whether the abortion happened 5, 10, 20, or 40 years earlier, some women carry shame and guilt with them as if it had happened only yesterday. They live in condemnation.

And there are other women who have had abortions who do not carry guilt or shame. They've written it off as a "necessary task." While they may think they were not, and are not, affected at all, really the abortion has been influencing many areas of their lives. It's their buried truth.

And that's why I'm writing this book—to share my "buried truth" about my abortions, my denial, and the process that God is using to set me free.

In this book, I expose the truth about abortion and its wounds so that you'll learn how to heal, and you'll realize the release of power to fully walk in the newness that Christ promised when we surrender to Him. And if you have not surrendered to Him, I will show you how to do that too.

MY STORY

My story is not an easy one to tell, especially when I think about how other people see me in my family, in my church, and in my community. I am a wife to a very successful man and mother to three very successful athletes. But, most importantly, I am the daughter of the most high God, and Christ is my Lord and Savior; therefore, I am obligated to shed my pride and share my story.

My story is one that truly glorifies what God can do when you trust Him. He is the answer to releasing us from the prison that abortion puts us in. And it is through Him, with Him, and by Him that I tell my story, so you too can find this release and fully walk in the newness of Christ. The way that the Lord heals you may not take the same path as mine. My story is evidence that He is real, and you can read it for inspiration, encouragement, and guidance.

SET YOU FREE

If you had an abortion in the past and you find yourself unable to check off that box when you go for your annual physical exam, the one that asks for the number of pregnancies you'd had in your lifetime, and you lie and exclude the pregnancies that were aborted—then this book will help set you free.

If you are still feeling guilty, beyond guilty, about the abortion(s)—then this book will help set you free.

If you think that you did not murder a baby, but just got rid of some tissue and no harm was done, then this book will help set you free.

If you had an abortion but, since then, were not able to have children when you wanted to have children, and you feel like that is your punishment for having the abortion(s)—then this book will help set you free.

RIGHT NOW

I ask you to seek your healing now, do not put it off any longer. Do not delay. Read this book now and allow the Holy Spirit to work in your life so that you can be healed. And not just healed, but equipped to work for the Lord in whatever area He is calling you.

In the times that we live in, the world needs to hear about our Savior. Don't let your past—your abortion—keep you silent anymore. Be healed and be used.

IN SUMMARY

The Lord has placed it on my heart to share my story so that you can be released from the emotions that are holding you captive because you had an abortion(s). Your healing may not look exactly like mine, but my story is here to show you that the Lord has forgiven you and He is real and ready and able to restore you fully.

INVITATION TO PONDER

For hope and healing, ponder these Scriptures:

- Psalm 147:3

- Hebrews 4:14–16

Also, consider the following:

- What would your life, both your interior and exterior life, be like if you did not hide that you had an abortion(s)? Imagine it. Write or Draw it. Express it.

MY THOUGHTS/FEELINGS

_____
_____
_____
_____
_____
_____
_____
_____
_____
_____
_____
_____
_____
_____
_____
_____
_____
_____
_____
_____
_____
_____
_____
_____
_____
_____
_____
_____
_____

Chapter 1

WOUNDS

When the Lord first gave me the concept for this book, He placed in my mind the title, *Forgiven: Healing the Wounds of Abortion with Christ*. Let's take a moment to explore that word "wounds."

When I think of a wound, I think of something physical. The word actually conjures up a vision of a man in battle and him being hurt badly. Or a puppy whose leg was hurt by another animal. Or falling off a bike and scraping a knee. My immediate association is not with abortion. Particularly, because I was of the mindset, like many, that abortion was a medical procedure, like getting your tonsils taken out. And, I do not think of medical procedures causing wounds. In fact, I see them as a means to cure people. So that idea that abortions create wounds was foreign to me.

Nevertheless, let's explore the word "wound" to see why it does apply to abortion and to understand that we do need to attend to this wound for it to be repaired.

PROBING THE WOUNDS

What is a wound?

According to *Merriam Webster's Dictionary* (2017) a "wound" is:

1. a. an injury to the body (as from violence, accident, or surgery)

that typically involves laceration or breaking of a membrane (as the skin) and usually damage to underlying tissues.
b. a cut or breach in a plant usually due to an external agent.

2.   a mental or emotional hurt or blow.

3.   something resembling a wound in appearance or effect; especially a rift in or blow to a political body or social group.

From its definition, we can surmise that a wound can be physical, emotional/mental, or symbolic.

The wounds of abortion comprise all three—a physical wound, an emotional wound, and a symbolic wound.

The Physical

First, an abortion manifests itself as a true physical wound—a true "laceration or breaking of a membrane" and "damage to underlying tissues." For the procedure to be "completed," that is necessarily what occurs.

One Saturday, a couple of weeks ago, I went over to my pastor's house for a discussion group. In the discussion, the topic of abortion came up. Our pastor told us that he had talked to people who were formerly involved in the abortion industry, and they told him that when women endured abortions, typically they screamed during the process. Women physically opened their mouths and let out screams. Thus, an abortion is a physical pulling out. It is a violent, physical injury to the body.

When our pastor shared that information, my mind instantly returned to my time on the table, the long scream that I released, and the crying, hurt, and pain. Yes, it was certainly a physically wounding act.

The Emotional

At the time of the abortion, women endure literal physical wounds. Over time, those physical wounds may heal; however, what remains in some women is an enduring mental/emotional wound. Abortions create mental/emotional blows that damage women's hearts and souls. Some know this well.

The emotional hurt is tangible. A woman confessed that one of her friends had had an abortion 40 years earlier, and the guilt still crippled the friend even though she was a follower of Jesus Christ. Depression engulfed the woman, and she felt her subsequent inability to conceive when she did want a child was her punishment for the abortion.

Other women have shared that after the abortion, their lives followed a path of drugs and alcohol to numb the shame, the pain, and the guilt. Others walk the path of promiscuity—which they may have already been on—but the abortion causes them to seek out sexual intimacy even more often to soothe themselves.

Others deny the emotional wound from their abortion, the emotional and mental wound that festers in them for years upon years. I was one of those.

But just because I said it did not bother me did not mean that the poison was not infecting my body, my pursuit of a purpose in life, or my family. For instance, I realized that stuffing the emotions around the abortions extended into other areas of my life where I simply had cut off emotions. The poison showed up as perpetual anger, sometimes rage.

I did not realize that there was a range of negative emotions due to those buried abortions that I drew upon when seemingly unrelated challenges arose. Anger seemed to be the only response available to me. Having abortions played a role in me developing this very one-dimensional emotional response. I had very deep feelings about the abortions that I had buried inside myself, and those feelings had to go somewhere, whether I wanted to acknowledge them or not.

The Symbolic

And, thirdly, abortion results in a symbolic wound. The Bible says that we, humans, are image bearers of God—the Father, Son, and Holy Spirit (Genesis 1:27). From this we can easily extrapolate that when a baby is aborted, the abortion that literally kills the baby equates to a symbolic killing of the image of God.

To repeat: when a woman gets an abortion, she's choosing to undergo a process that kills the image of God—symbolically— through the literally killing of the baby.

I know this is a serious claim. For someone already feeling guilty about her abortion, I am sure that you are saying, "How is this going to make me feel less guilt? You just said that I killed God's image."

Yes, I did, but bear with me. This is about exposing truth for the purpose of healing, not condemnation or destruction.

Trust me—but more importantly—trust God. God has carried me through this healing process and carefully led me through its unfolding, and now He wants me to share it with you. In reading this book and undergoing the process I'm laying out, you will find your path to restoration. So, again, trust God.

FIXING YOUR EYES ON JESUS

Abortion causes wounds—wounds that need to be administered to. The process by which these wounds will be mended may be, most likely, painful because you have to face something that you did not want to confront. I know that I sure did not. This healing process reminds me of the Scripture where Christ suffered knowing that He would rejoice in our salvation.

Fixing our eyes on Jesus, the Author and Perfecter of faith, Who for the joy set before Him endured the cross, despising the shame, and has sat down at the right hand of the throne of God.

—Hebrews 12:2

While Jesus endured excruciating physical suffering on the cross, all the while He had awareness and faith that the reward (the joy set before Him) that would result from His suffering would be so much greater than the suffering itself.

The same holds true for the repairing of our wounds. What we have avoided for so long—the shame, the guilt, revisiting the physical pain—will be unearthed, and it is not easy to face. Anger and sadness flooded me at times, I wanted to eat to stuff down the feelings that were coming up, and I wanted to quit the process. I wanted to quit writing this book.

Nonetheless, what I held onto, and I encourage you to hold onto, is the "joy set before" you. That is, the reward of being set free from the bondage of holding this secret. God brought this hurt to the light because it needed to be dealt with; He will be alongside you through the process; and we can fix our eyes on Jesus Christ as we go through it.

The Greek word for "fix "in this Scripture is *aphorao*, which means to turn your eyes away from other things and fix (direct your attention, mind) unwaveringly toward Jesus Christ. Prayer, worship, and reading the Bible is how I stayed fixed on Christ throughout this journey.

WOUNDS, ACCORDING TO ABORTION-RECOVERY LITERATURE

The wounds, physical, emotional, and symbolic, that I've been describing are REAL. In the scientific community, however, there is disagreement upon whether mental health problems/distress associated with abortion is legitimate. Some research has shown that post-abortive women have:

59% increased risk for suicidal thoughts

61% increased risk for mood disorders

61% increased social anxiety disorders

261% increase risk for alcohol abuse

280% risk for any substance use disorder[1]

Whereas, other research has concluded that there is no connection between abortion and subsequent mental health problems.[2] Every side—pro-abortion and pro-life—has a point to prove to the other. But for the purpose of healing—yours and mine—we must set aside the experts and acknowledge what we have felt and buried for too long.

You can read about the most common post-abortion wounds in the many books written about the abortion recovery process. Often in those books, there is a chapter where the author asks you to take a self-assessment regarding your "aftereffects" or wounds. The following is a summary of symptoms that the abortion recovery literature states that women may experience after having an abortion. Note: the intensity and variety of the symptoms often differs from woman to woman.

PHYSICAL SYMPTOMS

Miscarriage	Colon problems	Uterine scarring
Infertility	Long, difficult labor	Endometriosis
Sterility	Breast cancer	Infection
Stillbirth	Pelvic inflammatory disease	
Cervical pain	Irregular menstruation	

EMOTIONAL SYMPTOMS

Fear and anxiety

Avoidance of stimuli associated with the trauma

Regret and guilt

Difficulty recalling details of the abortion(s)

Sadness and sorrow

Denial of any emotions related to the abortion

Feelings of loss

Replacement baby feelings
(i.e., a strong urge to get pregnant and keep baby)

Repeat abortions

Heightening of pre-existing phobias

Sleep problems

Over-protectiveness of current children

Promiscuity

Inability to make good decisions

Numbing of emotions

Difficulty in intimate relationships

Emotional pain

Eating disorder, like anorexia or bulimia

Nightmares

Drug and alcohol abuse

Shame

Self-destructive behavior

Anger and rage

Suicidal impulses

Desire for secrecy about abortion

IN SUMMARY

Having an abortion creates a wound in our body—a physical, emotional, and symbolic wound. Some wounds heal on their own, like paper cuts, scrapes on the knees, stubbing a toe against the door; but more intense wounds require attention so that they can be mended properly. An abortion creates an intense wound as supported by the abortion recovery literature, something which you know from your own experience. Acknowledging that is the first step to restoration.

As I felt led by the Lord in this healing process, it became clear to me that my next step was to explore wounds that were in my life even before I had my first abortion.

INVITATION TO PONDER

For hope and healing, ponder this Scripture:

- Hebrews 12:2

Also, consider the following:

- After reflecting upon what you just read, what can you identify as your "aftereffects" or wounds from having an abortion(s)?

MY WOUNDS

_____
_____
_____
_____
_____
_____
_____
_____
_____
_____
_____
_____
_____
_____
_____
_____
_____
_____
_____
_____
_____
_____
_____
_____
_____
_____
_____

Chapter 2

WOUNDS FROM BEFORE

Before I had an abortion, I was already living with many wounds. Perhaps you're wondering—why would I explore these wounds from so long ago? Am I going to be digging up the past for the purpose of blaming? Am I trying to absolve myself of the guilt and responsibility for what I chose to do with three of my babies? What is the purpose?

When I think of the purpose of looking at my pre-abortion wounds, I think of a car. Now, I don't know much about cars, but I definitely can distinguish between a new car and an old one that's not working properly. When my car is not functioning, I take it to the manufacturer's service department. They know all about the car because they made it, so they can diagnose and fix it.

Before my first abortion, I was a car in need of repair. I was born into sin because I was born into a world that is sin-sick due to the break in humanity's relationship with God that took place in the garden. As a newborn baby, I needed a Savior, but I didn't know that then, and I proceeded through life taking on more and more events that continued to pile up the sin.

Continuing this metaphor, we could say that immediately when I got off the manufacturing line, I was a car with service issues. (For that matter, all cars getting off the line were in need of service. See Romans 3:23) But, rather than getting service, I drove around acquiring more and more damage, still in dire need of repair.

The purpose of uncovering these old wounds is like the diagnostic that the car dealer performs before beginning the car repair. Determining the disrepair—the wounds—is my way of bringing the car to the manufacturer's service department—God—so that He can fix me. I can let go, no more do-it-yourself healing.

As you read about my pre-abortion wounds, if emotions or thoughts are stirred regarding your history, please jot them down in this book, on your smartphone, on a piece of paper, or in a journal. In the way that suits you best, you are making note of how God is speaking to you.

OLD WOUND—MY FATHER AND I

I am so sick of that same old love. The kind that breaks your heart . . .
I am so sick of that same old love . . .

—Selena Gomez

My journey to the abortion clinic, the first time and subsequent times after, began way before that day in June 1986—it began at my conception. Let me explain . . .

When I hear the lyrics to "Same Old Love," Selena Gomez's song, pictures of my father flash through my head. The song describes the love that the singer experiences over and over again from men—different men. Though it is a love she experiences from different men, it is always the same in that it is a love that hurts and crushes her. It's a destructive cycle.

Perhaps, it seems odd that I would think about my father when I hear these painful lyrics. Perhaps it seems odd that the song doesn't conjure up an image of a lost love or an unrequited love, and, instead, I think of my father.

During a phone conversation with a friend, I mentioned that in my 48 years of life my father has never called to wish me happy birthday. My friend responded, "Why would he wish you happy birthday? He wasn't happy that you were born."

Wow—the statement stung, but . . . that seemed to be the case.

From the evidence of how my father has interacted with me over the years it would seem that he, indeed, was not happy that I was born. I would go so far as to say that it felt like he wished that I was never born. I do not have proof of that, but that's what the evidence suggests. From the stories that I was told, he liked my mother some 49 years ago, but a baby was not part of the deal.

Here are the thoughts that have circulated in my head over the course of my life:

My father never wanted me. He never was able to get over the fact that he did not plan for me, so he was never a father who was present. He had another woman waiting in the wing when he was through with my mother. These thoughts shaped the kind of love that I repeatedly went after in men.

I kept longing for that love from my father that never happened, and it drove me to repeatedly seek connection with unavailable males. As cliché as it sounds, it is true. My desire for my father to say that he loved me and that he was proud of me and that he was happy that God blessed him with me—that yearning—drove me into the paths of men who, also, could have cared less about me. I was always trying to make some guy like me. And the babies that I aborted became the causalities of that "same old love," that dusty, broken, cracked, worn-out love.

Currently, I talk to my father about once every six months when I call him. He rarely, if ever, since I have become an adult, calls me.

Six months ago when I was having a casual conversation with my father, he mentioned a conversation that took place between him and one of his other adult children. In this conversation, the adult child questioned whether I was truly my father's biological daughter.

The complication of the situation that I was born into is that my father was separated or divorced—the story is not clear—from his wife when I was conceived. Not only did he have a wife, but they had children.

In my opinion, his children have struggled all of their childhood and, apparently, their adult life with the fact that I am "their" father's daughter. We all grew up in the same small town, and the whispers of "Am I 'their' father's daughter?" were heard in the corners of the hallways of elementary school, junior high, high school, basketball games, friends' houses, etc. The whispers followed me like a haunting wind throughout my childhood and teenage years.

My father's parents raised me, from the time that I was a year old until I graduated from high school, so it was always peculiar that my father questioned my paternity, considering I lived with his mother and father. It was confusing for me, and hurtful, but I put on a great mask. I did not need his love nor did I need his children or his wife's acceptance. I had a "Mama" and a "Daddy," my grand-parents.

Looking back, I created a brick wall around my heart, and I seemed to only let in male companions who really did not like me. What a paradox! I was hurting and in need of nurturing and caring, and I only allowed males close to me who were guaranteed to stomp all over me, figuratively. That's the "same old love" I was used to.

As I mentioned, my paternal grandparents reared me. I did not grow up with my father or my mother. Growing up, I would de-scribe my relationship with my mother as strained. We were friend-ly on and off. Actually, during one of our "off" moments, she told me that she'd tried to abort me, but it hadn't worked.

Despite the ugly moments in my childhood and adolescence—and potentially wounding moments—over the years my mother and I have become closer, especially since my grandparents have died. One of the many things that I admire about my mother is that she is grateful to my grandparents for raising me, and she is quick to admit that they did a great job parenting me, a better job than she could have.

RESURFACING OF OLD WOUNDS

I shared with my mother the conversation that my father had told me about—his adult child doubting that he is my father. In addition, I casually stated, "If my father still has doubts after all this time that I am his daughter, then maybe we should take a DNA test" (although I knew that I would NOT take a DNA test at such a late stage in the game).

Heat and daggers flew out of my mother's mouth.

My response: confusion.

Why was she so angry? To me, a DNA test did not question my mother's integrity or reputation. Also, it was 48 years ago, so it didn't matter—right? My mother was behaving like she was 20 years old all over again. Words spewed out of her mother like snake venom.

She told me how my father had tried to discourage other men from dating her—although he was not interested in her himself. She explained, "He told someone, 'You don't want to talk to her. You know, she has a baby.' " The baby my father was referring to was me.

My mother then revealed the biggest shocker of all—"Your father has already taken a DNA test for you years ago. The test proved you are his biological daughter with a 99.9% accuracy rate."

My reaction—UTTER DISBELIEF. HURT—but I held in my emotions. My mother had enough emotion flowing that I didn't need to add to the brewing pot.

JOURNEY TO HEALING

Inside, my heart felt crushed yet again. Here I was at 48 years old, still feeling that pit in my stomach when it came to facing head-on the rejection that I felt my father had for me. I wondered, "Why didn't my father say to his other children that he knows, without a doubt, that I am his daughter? Why didn't he stand up for me?"

I've come up with some "answers" to these questions, some

reasons explaining his behavior—(1) because my father is now in his 70s, maybe he really doesn't remember; or (2) maybe he has blocked it out. But honestly, the reason doesn't matter.

In order for me to heal these old wounds, I simply must feel the hurt, acknowledge the hurt, and then work to understand how these hurtful emotions have controlled my thoughts and played out in my life.

This rejection that I've contended with all my life has not held me back from succeeding in many areas. I have not used it as a crutch. In some ways, I've even used it as a ladder to be all I could be, but . . . I recognized that it was time to find peace with my past, God's peace, not my manufactured-by-positive-thinking peace.

And, in order to have that peace, I had to acknowledge the feelings that I had buried all my life so that I could finally . . . BREATHE.

Before Christ, I could not face the hurt. The hurt was so huge, enormous—like Goliath to David. The hurt was a giant. If I ever would have let go and cried, I would have drowned in my tears. Now, however, it was clear—no more denying. In my denying, I was keeping that part of my life tucked away from God, even though He already knew, and I was not giving Him permission to let the Blood of Christ wash over it and cleanse it. It was not my burden to bear anymore.

Also, I had to let go of any ill feelings toward my father. The Bible says in Matthew 6:14–15 (Amplified Version):

> *For if you forgive others their trespasses [their reckless and willful sins], your heavenly Father will also forgive you. But if you do not forgive others [nurturing your hurt and anger with the result that*

it interferes with your relationship with God], then your Father will not forgive your trespasses.

I had to forgive my father. Forgiveness is an essential component of the healing process that I will discuss in the book.

In Accepting Jesus as Our Savior . . .

Over the years, in studying several books of the Bible, I have learned what God says about me now that I have accepted Jesus Christ as my Savior.

When I read 2 Corinthians 5:17:

Therefore if any man be in Christ, he is a new creature: old things are passed away; behold, all things are become new. (King James Version)

I take away that—I am a new creature in Christ.

When I read 1 John 1:7:

But if we (really) walk in the Light (that is, live each and every day in conformity with the precepts of God), as He Himself is in the Light, we have (true, unbroken) fellowship with one another (He with us, and we with Him), and the blood of Jesus His Son cleanses us from all sin (by erasing the stain of sin, keeping us cleansed from sin in all its forms and manifestations). (Amplified)

I take away that—*The Blood of Jesus Christ has cleansed me from all my sins.*

These takeaways are so momentous, so important for me—and for you—that I want to repeat them again. Let's let it really sink in. When we accept Jesus Christ as our Savior:

- *We are new creatures in Christ.*

- *The Blood of Jesus Christ cleanses us from all our sins.*

This is the truth that needs to sink into my head and my heart. This is the truth that needs to sink into your head and your heart too.

We all have some circumstance that laid the pathway to the abortion clinic. We all had some wound(s) before we submitted ourselves to lie on that table. That is fact, not justification, just fact.

It is time to take off the mask of "Everything has always been okay with me. I am strong." The Word of God says—*In our weakness, He, the Lord is strong.*

The Word also says—*Cast our cares unto Him because He cares for you. I am continually casting my cares unto Him. He is strong and He can carry the load of our cares and sins.*

IN SUMMARY

Uncovering factors related to your abortion is like weeding a garden: if you only take a part of the weed out, it looks like it is gone, but it will grow back and choke your harvest. So, like with weeding, in this process you must expose all factors that the Lord shows you so that your wounds are destroyed at the root. For me, this included processing some very painful memories, some of which happened years before the abortions themselves, as well as the circumstances around and memories of my abortions, which I'll share in the next chapter.

INVITATION TO PONDER

For hope and healing, ponder these Scriptures:

- 2 Corinthians 5:17

- 2 Corinthians 12:9–11

- 1 Peter 5:7

Also, consider the following:

- What emotions, thoughts, and recollections arise as you read this chapter? What cares do you need to give to the Lord?

MY THOUGHTS/FEELINGS

_____

_____

_____

_____

_____

_____

_____

_____

_____

_____

_____

_____

_____

_____

Chapter 3

WOUNDS FROM AFTER

ABOUT THE FIRST

At 19 years old, I aborted my first baby. The father of that baby had been my boyfriend for about eight months. After we discovered that I was pregnant, I don't remember our conversation about what to do about it, but I remember that at the end of the semester when I went home from college, I scheduled an appointment for an abortion.

I told my grandmother what I was going to do before I did it. I remember her eyes more than her words. Her eyes looked at me with such sympathy. I don't know if it was sympathy for the baby, for me, for her, or for all of us. I don't know what her eyes meant, but I remember feeling love from her—and not judgment.

After returning from the clinic, sadness overwhelmed me. I cried, and I was bleeding. I called the father of the baby that I'd just aborted, and he wasn't interested in talking to me. HURT. DISBELIEF. ANGER. HATRED—these are the feelings that arose in me at that moment.

When I returned to school that fall, he had moved on. He'd started dating another girl on campus. It was so painful to see him with her. I remember going to my best friend's dorm room where I cried with all that I had within me. I cried my guts out. Every ounce of hurt I may have stored up from every experience of abandonment and rejection, I vomited it out at that moment.

My friend and her boyfriend at the time thought that someone had died in my family. The pain was so visceral. I actually frightened them. I frightened myself.

I had never, to that point in my life, let out how I really felt about situations. I put up a front like I was tough. I would be angry, but NEVER cry out of pain. This time though, I could not hold it in.

ABOUT THE SECOND

I was 22 years old. This situation was somewhat different from the first one in that the father of the second child had not been in my life as consistently as the first one. So, I guess it did not hurt as much when he turned his back on me.

I'd been living in New Jersey but was moving back to the Midwest to attend graduate school. Before starting graduate school, I made a pit stop in my hometown of Battle Creek.

On this particular day, my biological father had invited me out to lunch. We were eating at one of my father's favorite burger restaurants. In the middle of our conversation, I felt this sudden urge to vomit. I rushed from the table and ran to the restroom. I returned to the table and was a bit confused about what had just happened. I was not sick, so that sudden urge did not make sense to me.

I described this experience to one of my girlfriends, and she told me that I was probably pregnant. I was.

I called father number 2 to tell him the news, and he instantly jumped defensive, telling me that if I was pregnant, he was not the father.

Definitely not the response I was looking for . . .

My response to his rejection—RESIGNED. NUMB. I was not shocked. I knew what I had to do.

I had to make a trip to the clinic . . . again.

For a brief moment, I wondered, "What would it mean to keep the baby?" I called a pregnancy crisis center to inquire about the kinds of assistance they could give me if I had a baby. They informed me that they could give me—clothing.

Clothing?

That was it.

"What's clothing going to help if I have a baby—without a job, without a man, and without his family to love the baby. I don't have anything to give the baby"—at least that was what I was thinking.

I did not want to bring a baby into the world where her father did not even acknowledge her. I knew the pain that caused—firsthand . . . And, in my mind, that was worse than not giving her a chance to live. (I know that this baby was a girl. God revealed that to me recently. I will share that later.)

So, with all these thoughts swirling in my head, I told one of my girlfriends and she took me to the clinic.

MORE SCREAMS AND TEARS.

I never heard from father 2 again.

My feelings—ISOLATED but LOVED by my friends.

ABOUT THE THIRD

I was 23 years old. I was in graduate school, studying to get my PhD in clinical psychology. People liked to tell me their problems, and I listened and advised well, so I thought I should pursue counseling as a career.

I met father 3 in graduate school. Our relationship was intense, right from the beginning. As I reflect back, we both really wanted to be loved by someone, so we jumped into a serious relationship with the words "I love you" really early on.

When I found myself in the now familiar situation of being faced with an unplanned pregnancy, I told him. His direction was different from the previous two. He immediately said that he was against abortion, and we needed to find another option.

My response—DISTRUST.

He asked me to call his parents and talk with them. I called. His mother asked me to have the baby and give it to them to rear. She and her husband would take care of the baby until I finished school.

Again, on my part—DISTRUST.

I did not know them. I did not know how they would care for the baby. What if they let someone molest him or beat him or verbally abuse him?

FEAR.

My life experiences led me to negative thoughts before I ever considered the magnitude of the positive offer they were laying before me.

I left their offer on the table, and I headed to the clinic.

Surprisingly enough, father 3 did not desert me. Nevertheless, I felt his love was not great enough to help me through a pregnancy, so our son suffered by dying at the hand of the abortionist, upon my request.

Baby
No tears,
I didn't know him-- ⇥
Or was it a her?
I didn't feel then-- ⇥
Or did I?
I cried with
Pain.
But we had to continue,
No turning back.
Then another.
I don't remember.
The third, I had to go back.
Not correct procedure.
I cried in the car.
Random man,
Random act of kindness,
"Sista, are you alright?"
Why could the father not
Love me like that?

WOUND INVENTORY

My wounds post-abortion: HURT, DISBELIEF, ANGER, HA-TRED, NUMBNESS, RESIGNATION, FEAR, DISTRUST (x 2).

I carried these wounds with me, but I pretended they did not exist. They have been having their way in my life because I didn't know—or didn't acknowledge—that they lingered.

They were taking control of my life. So, something had to give. Something had to change.

IN SUMMARY

There is a story attached to each abortion to which I consent-ed. Remembering brings to the surface the emotions—the weeds—that need to be destroyed. Handing them over to God, to no longer hide or dwell on them, in turn, has cleared that space for God to nurture those wounded areas.

INVITATION TO PONDER

For hope and healing, ponder this Scripture:

- Psalm 103:1–5

Also, consider the following:

- What is your story?
- What are the emotions tied to your story that you need to acknowledge and give to God?

MY STORY

_____

_____

_____

_____

_____

_____

_____

_____

_____

_____

_____

_____

_____

_____

_____

_____

_____

_____

_____

_____

_____

_____

_____

_____

_____

_____

_____

_____

_____

_____

_____

_____

_____

_____

_____

_____

_____

_____

_____

_____

_____

_____

_____

_____

_____

_____

_____

_____

_____

_____

_____

_____

_____

_____

_____

_____

Chapter 4

FROM MOCHA MOMS TO MIRACLE

At the age of 35, a miracle happened in my life. Ever since I was a teenager, I analyzed things in my life and others' lives, and always tried to find ways to improve. Searching to fill the holes in my heart and find love and belonging, I read self-help books and joined organizations.

In 2002, I joined a group called Mocha Moms. The founders of Mocha Moms designed the organization to support black women who had chosen to be mothers who stayed at home instead of working in the marketplace. At the age of 35, I was a stay-at-home wife and mother of three sons, ages 10, 5, and 2.

At a Mocha Moms meeting, one of the ladies asked me to deliver a cake to her sister-in-law who lived near me. The Mocha Moms group that I attended was in Philadelphia, Pennsylvania, about 45 minutes from my home in New Jersey. The sister-in-law lived in New Jersey not far from me. I volunteered to drop off the cake, and the sister-in-law and I instantly connected.

Over the course of our friendship, I asked the sister-in-law to come to a Creative Memories workshop that I was hosting. She agreed. So, when she asked me to come to a women's conference at her church, I felt obligated to attend. Little did I know, but God had a treat waiting for me at that conference.

The speaker at the conference, Faith (not her real name, but I will refer to her as such going forward), was a very powerful woman of God. That is, she was very clear about her purpose in Christ. When I heard her speak, something inside of me jumped—something like butterflies but less fluttery and more like a quick jump (I did not know at the time, but it was my inner spirit man). My reaction signified to me that she and I would work together.

Faith was speaking of Shiphrah and Puah, the two Hebrew midwives, from the Bible:

> *Then the king of Egypt spoke to the Hebrew midwives, one of whom was named Shiphrah and the other was named Puah; and he said, "When you are helping the Hebrew women to give birth and see them upon the birthstone, if it is a son, then you shall put him to death; but if it is a daughter, then she shall live." But the midwives feared God, and did not do as the king of Egypt had commanded them, but let the boys live.*
>
> —Exodus 1:15–17

As I listened to Faith, I sensed that she and I would birth something together, but I did not know what.

Soon after that, I began attending a women's Bible study that Faith hosted and facilitated from her house. I had not surrendered my life to Christ, but I was learning more and more about God and Christ and the Holy Spirit. Let me note too that as I write this, I realize that once "I found" the Bible study, I no longer attended meetings for Mocha Moms, and I bought fewer self-help books. Interesting . . . my searching for belonging and purpose seemed to be fulfilled when I began to learn more about God.

About four months or so after joining the Bible study, my marriage hit a large bump—a crisis of sorts.

And then the miracle happened.

My good friend, Hope, who is a born-again believer in Jesus Christ, talked to me during this time.

One day over the phone as I lamented about my problems, Hope asked, "Do you believe in Jesus Christ?"

Instantly, my defenses flew up. I'd grown up in the church. Pastor Chandler had baptized me when I was 11 years old. How could she ask me if I knew Jesus Christ? She was starting to sound like Mrs. Harrison, my neighbor in my hometown who had told me so blatantly—"You do NOT believe in Christ."

What was wrong with these women?

I told Hope, with much attitude in my voice, "I know Jesus Christ. I go to church. I hear the sermons. I think that means I know Christ."

In reality, the evidence that I spit out to Hope did not mean that I believed in Jesus Christ. I was ignorant to that fact.

It was after that conversation that I realized Hope and Mrs. Harrison were both right. I did not believe in Christ. So, I surrendered my life to Christ.

FROM THE MOMENT OF SURRENDER

. . . That if you confess with your mouth Jesus as Lord, and believe in your heart that God raised Him from the dead, you will be saved; for with the heart a person believes, resulting in righteousness, and with the mouth he confesses, resulting in salvation.

—Romans 10:9—10

When I surrendered my life to Christ, I do not remember if I stated the exact words of Roman 10. Nevertheless, I surrendered my life to Christ, and He gave me His salvation.

It did not happen in church. It happened in my house and in my heart.

According to Hebrews 10:12 and 14, " . . . but He, having offered one sacrifice for sins for all time, sat down at the right hand of God . . . For by one offering He has perfected for all time those who are sanctified." And Psalm 103: 12 states, "As far as the east is from the west, so far has He removed our transgressions from us."

With these Scriptures in mind—at that moment when I surrendered to Christ, stating, "You are Lord, Lord of my life," I was cleansed of all my sins. All my sins. ALL. All means all. I became a new creature. That is what His Word says, "Therefore if any man be in Christ, he is a new creature: old things are passed away; behold, all things are become new" (2 Corinthians 5:17, KJV).

S0—I was new.

I am new.

TRANSFORMING TO NEW

Gladys Smith, a Christian woman I met years ago, told me that the Lord transforms us sometimes immediately, and in some areas it is layer by layer because we cannot handle a full and total transformation all at once. And that's how it unfolded with me.

Change: Hungering for God's Word

The immediate change was my thirst for the Word of God. I

hungered for His Word, more and more. I was already participating in studying the Bible with Faith. We focused on topical studies, such as looking at women in the Bible.

Next, the Lord led me to Greater Life Church with Pastor Chris Love. Pastor Love is a man of God who LOVES the Word of God and worship. With Pastor Love, I continued to learn more and more about who God—the Father, Son, and Holy Spirit—is. I was not only hearing it from the Pastor's mouth, but also we were looking and digging into the Word on Sundays and Wednesdays.

When my family and I moved to California, the Lord continued to pour in me this hunger for Him and His Word. I ended up in a Precepts Bible Study that met once a week. And, in order to complete our work for the next meeting, the study required reading, studying, and interacting with the Word of God five days a week. The Word had become like food for me. Just as I ate food daily, I ate the Word of God daily, with a break on weekends (I am working towards seven days a week).

My point is that the Lord had, and has, me in His Word regularly and consistently.

Precept Bible Studies are not cursory glances over the Word. You really dig deep into the Word for the purpose of knowing God and applying His Word to your life. The first Precept Bible Study that I completed focused on the Book of John. It required 18 months for us to complete that study—18 months. That is a full year and six months on one book of the Bible—intense study.

God was transforming me through His Word. The changes to the naked eye were not dramatic at first—my husband will attest to that. However, my oldest son, who was 10 years old when I surrendered my life, noticed that I had become a new creature—not perfect, but being perfected, and new.

Change: Hungering to Share God's Greatness

As I said, I hungered for God's Word, I hungered for His righteousness, and I hungered to tell people of God's greatness. I wanted to tell people what He had done for me and how He is available to them.

With Faith's Bible study, she required us to serve the local community. We would feed people and give clothes and Bibles. I remember on one of these outings, walking around with a man who was not saved, but he was helping us gather people from the neighborhood to come to the park, where they could eat and select from clothes we had provided what they needed. It was a great time where I shared my testimony and talked to him about his life.

Change: Hungering to Educate My Children

I also began to homeschool our three sons at this same time. This is a direction to which the Holy Spirit had DEFINITELY directed me. Before being saved, I had NO desire to homeschool our children. My thoughts about homeschooling before Christ were "What for? There are all kinds of schools to choose from—no reason to do that."

But the Lord had other plans . . .

Moreover, I will give you a new heart and put a new spirit within you; and I will remove the heart of stone from your flesh and give you a heart of flesh.

—Ezekiel 36:26

Changed my black heart into Gold.

—Jess Glynne, "My Love"

So, the Lord was changing me and using me. Even still, He had not brought to my attention yet the wounds of abortion that were inside of me—but that was about to happen . . . in a very subtle fashion.

IN SUMMARY

For as long as I can remember, I felt a constant pull to belong and feel loved. I constantly examined myself to see where I could improve and make myself better emotionally. I guess, so I would be perfect and people would like and accept me.

When I surrendered my life to Jesus Christ that hole for acceptance and love finally began to be filled. Giving my life to Christ and studying His Word started the process for God to make monumental changes in my life, the kind that I had been wanting (that were the reasons behind my whole self-help odyssey) but could never seem to make happen on my own.

I had found what I had been searching for—what wonderful news. It would not be right to keep this good news to myself. Nevertheless, I had no plan for sharing the good news of Jesus Christ, but God did have a plan.

INVITATION TO PONDER

For hope and healing, ponder these Scriptures:

- Romans 10:9–10

- Romans 12:1–2

- Ezekiel 36:26

Also, consider the following:

- Are you a follower of Jesus Christ? Have you surrendered your life to Christ?

- Do you spend time in His Word—the Holy Bible?

MY RELATIONSHIP WITH CHRIST & HIS WORD

_____
_____
_____
_____
_____
_____
_____
_____
_____
_____
_____
_____
_____
_____
_____
_____
_____
_____

Chapter 5

AT THE CENTER OF THE LABYRINTH

As I mentioned in the introduction of this book, in the first Bible study I attended with Faith, several women, including me, confessed that we had aborted babies. We confessed it to one another and did not discuss it again. It was an open and shut case. Our past was covered in the Blood of Jesus' sacrifice for all of our sins, once and for all. That was true, and, at that time, that was as deep as the Lord wanted me to explore it.

In California, I attended a church that hosted an abortion recovery Bible study. I mentioned the study to a friend, who had never aborted a child, that maybe I should attend the group. She encouraged me to forget that idea because it was clear to her that I was walking with the Lord, and there was not a need to discuss the issue. She was correct: I was walking with the Lord, and I did know clearly that He had forgiven me, so I did not attend the study. Again, the subject of abortion in my past was opened and shut.

Later, I moved to Indiana. It was there, in Indiana, that the Lord clearly began to speak to me that it was time that I uncovered the wounds from abortion to allow healing to take place and to share with other women, so they can be free.

The timespan between giving my life to the Lord and this revelation that it was time to expose the wounds of abortion was 10 years.

10 years.

I had been saved 10 years before God allowed me to delve into these wounds.

Why so long? Because my delving into the wounds is not just for the sake of having pity, wallowing in past sin, or even glorifying past sin—its purpose is to glorify God.

It took 10 years for me to be ready to probe and expose these abortion wounds so that I could do so for the purpose of glorifying God by sharing God's message with others. God's message that I'm sharing—

He saved me, He is changing me! I am a new creature because of Him. I am talking about the aborting of three of my children so that people can know how forgiving and full of loving kindness God truly is. He is mercy and grace and truth. He is Love.

HOW THE CHANGE UNFOLDED

In Indiana, Lifecare, a pro-life pregnancy center, invited one of the pastors from our church, Pastor Hannah, to lead a prayer at their annual dessert event. Pastor Hannah's husband could not attend the event, so he prompted her to ask me to attend with her.

Supporting a pro-life organization was not on my radar at that time. While I had nothing against supporting a pro-life organization, it just was not something that I, personally, had considered doing. After asking the Holy Spirit what reason I had to attend such an event, I hesitantly accepted Pastor Hannah's invitation. After that event, I also attended a banquet hosted by Lifecare.

At these two events, I heard the testimonies of young women who had chosen to give life to their babies instead of aborting them, despite their circumstances. These testimonies stirred sadness, guilt, and joy inside of me. I felt joy because they had the courage to give their babies life and sad and guilty because I had not done that.

I hadn't even realized that the guilt was inside of me. God had forgiven me, so I had thought the guilt had been dissolved. However, I was wrong, and God knew that. He knew I needed to be free.

After the banquet, I met with the director of Lifecare to volunteer as a post-abortion recovery counselor. I thought that I could empathize with the women who had aborted their babies and assist them in seeing God's grace and forgiveness. I did not end up counseling because of the time commitment. Apparently God had another plan for my involvement with Lifecare.

When I was out walking in my neighborhood, I saw a lady whom I had never seen before. I felt the Holy Spirit telling me to talk to her, but fear caused me to hesitate. By the time I mustered up the courage to go and talk with her, she had disappeared behind her house.

I told the Lord that I would figure out a way to talk to her, so I brainstormed ideas of how I would meet her. I thought, "Maybe, I'll bring her a cake to welcome her to the neighborhood." But I did not have to design a strategy because the Lord worked it out.

One Saturday in Wal-Mart, I saw her. I rushed up to her and asked if she lived on my street. She said yes, and we began to talk. In the conversation, she told me that her name was Abigail, and she had been visiting a church in town—it happened to be my church.

What a coincidence—not really. There are no coincidences in God.

I told her the next time that she visited she should sit with my family. So, over the next four weeks or so, we sat together in church and talked briefly after service.

One Sunday after church as we were walking out, Ms. Abigail told me that she was a board member of an organization, she was retiring, and she wondered if I was interested in replacing her. That organization was Lifecare.

The request overwhelmed me, and I said I would pray about it, hoping the Lord would say that it was not a good idea.

The next week, Ms. Abigail told me that she had informed the director of Lifecare that she had selected someone to replace her. Before Ms. Abigail could tell the director that it was me, the director told her that she too had found someone to replace her. When they shared their names, they both said—my name. That was confirmation to me that I needed to sit on the Lifecare board.

In 2014, a friend of mine in California asked me to be the keynote speaker for a homeschool conference for an organization of which we were both members. Both excitement and anxiety filled me. I was not sure if I would be able to do it even though the organization that hosted the conference would train me.

Despite my uncertainty, I agreed to be the keynote speaker. My talk ended up being very interactive because that is the kind of teacher that God made me. It is very difficult for me to lecture. I need feedback—conversation—to facilitate learning.

That year the focus of the conference was the "Art of Rhetoric:

Cultivating the Conversation." During the break, one of the conference participants gently walked up to me and said how happy she was to see someone of color speaking to the group. She felt people needed to see people of color involved in key positions in the homeschool movement. At the end of our little chat, she handed me a newspaper/magazine booklet. I did not look at it at that moment because I was scheduled to speak again.

When I arrived at my hotel room, I looked at the newspaper. It was actually an advertising supplement, Did You Know?,[3] and it was totally dedicated to informing readers on how abortion had negatively impacted the black community. Unbelievable. I had not even been speaking about abortion. I had been discussing the art of rhetoric. Why would this woman give this information to me?

In August 2014, two months after my speaking engagement, I felt that I needed refreshing before I started the new homeschool year, so I decided to go on a retreat by myself. I searched on the Internet and found a house in Michigan that sat by a lake on 70 acres of land. It was designated for Christian spiritual retreats. Groups or individuals could use the house. I booked the room for 2 days and 1 night. There was no TV, no Internet, no traffic—just me, my Bible, and the Lord.

There was one other guest situated in a separate house on the property. The quiet and solitude were deafening. It screamed so loudly as compared to the backdrop of the busyness of my daily life—with my husband, my sons, my house, and meeting the needs of others engulfing my life.

The quiet frightened me. I slept with a light on. The next morning, I explored the property and discovered a prayer labyrinth. A labyrinth is like a maze except there are no dead ends down the paths. In a labyrinth, there is one path, so although it seems like you are only going in circles, you are always moving and moving to the center.

The instructions for using a prayer labyrinth are simple: pray and walk. As I began to walk, I thanked God for being who He is, the One who created the heavens, the earth, the sea, and all that is within them. I thanked Christ for being my Savior and for going to the cross for me, and I thanked Holy Spirit for being my Teacher and Comforter. I walked and walked, and a burning question rose up in me: "What am I to write about?"

People had told me many times in my life that I would write a book, and I always desired to write a book. I loved reading books as a child. So, here I was walking, and I felt my inner man ask the Lord, "What will I write my book about?" I heard clearly in my spirit that the book was to focus on how He had forgiven me for the abortions that I had. I just started crying and crying, but I kept walking and I made it to the center.

It was clear from then on that I would write this book. It was also clear to me that when God says He forgives all sins, He does mean all. He forgave my aborting my babies.

For by one offering He has perfected forever and completely cleansed those who are being sanctified [bringing each believer to spiritual completion and maturity]. And the Holy Spirit also adds His testimony to us [in confirmation of this]; for after having said,

"This is the covenant that I will make them After those days, says the Lord: I will imprint My laws upon their heart, And on their mind I will inscribe them [producing an inward change],"

He then says,

"And their sins and their lawless acts I will remember no more [no longer holding their sins against them]."

—Hebrews 10:14–17 (Amplified Version) [words bolded by author]

And it was clear to me that this book was going to be a vehicle for me to share the good news of Jesus Christ.

ABRAHAM, ISAAC, AND ME

I regretted that I aborted my children, and I felt guilty. I felt ashamed. God asked me to lay it all on the altar for Him, similarly to how He'd asked Abraham to lay Isaac on the altar. Abraham truly loved Isaac, his firstborn child. He had waited until he was 100 years old before Isaac was conceived. Abraham could have idolized Isaac. He could have worshiped and adored Isaac over God. So, when God asked Abraham to sacrifice Isaac, God wanted to see if Abraham loved Him more than Isaac.

Abraham was obedient to God. He loved God more. And he knew that God knew he loved Isaac; and he knew that God had given him prophecies about Isaac, so he knew that God would work it out somehow. Abraham was just going to be obedient, trust God, and watch God work it out.

When I compare my situation to Abraham's, it is not that I adore or worship that I had three abortions. Instead, it is like I worship and adore how other people see me—my image—as a woman who loves the Lord and His Word, who is holy and righteous in Christ, and who is loving and kind.

By telling my story and exposing my wounds, I do not know how it will affect relationships I have with people. People whom I love may not be able to handle what I did. People in my community may no longer see me as a devout Christian woman.

Nevertheless, I have to be like Abraham and trust God because I do love God above all else in my life. And I know that if He has asked me to do, it is for my good and His good, and He will provide me a way of escape just like He provided Abraham that ram in the bush.

So, I move forward.

God in the Bible is the same God who is in our lives right now. He is Healer, Redeemer, Provider, Love, All-knowing.

IN SUMMARY

I had been a follower of Jesus Christ for 10 years before the Lord prompted me to look at the aftereffects of my abortions. On each of our walks with Christ, at God's appointed time, issues will arise that are important for us to examine so that we mature in the Lord. It was not clear to me why my abortions were the chosen vehicle (through this book) for sharing the good news of Christ, but I had to be obedient. The result of my obedience was more work on me before I even started to type one word of the book.

INVITATION TO PONDER

To encourage you when you feel like stopping your digging up of the weeds around abortion, ponder these Scriptures:

- 1 Samuel 15: 22
- James 1:2–4
- 1 John 2: 5-6

Also, consider the following:

- **Reflect upon how you came to read this book.**
- What events or people in your life have pointed you to begin to address your past abortion(s)?
- Note: Answering the above question will show you how God is involved in this process. You are not alone.

MY REFLECTIONS

_____
_____
_____
_____
_____
_____
_____
_____
_____
_____
_____
_____

_____

_____

_____

_____

_____

_____

_____

_____

_____

_____

_____

_____

_____

_____

_____

_____

_____

_____

_____

_____

_____

_____

_____

_____

_____

Chapter 6

CRACKING APART THE WALLS

After my solo retreat in 2014, the Lord has been chiseling the hardness off of my heart. Even though I know that I received a new heart when I was 35 and said that Jesus could come into my heart, there have been places that were still rough. Yet, God has been gentle in removing that roughness. In the last two years, the chiseling has become more intense.

To support me with the intensity, James 1:3 reminds me that we face trial and tribulations in order to be perfected into the image of Christ. And I know that the finished perfection does not happen until we see Jesus Christ, either through earthly death or His second return. God is not done with me yet, even as I write about how He has been healing me. He will continue to perfect me until I see Him (this is called Progressive Sanctification. I will discuss it further in Chapter 7).

THE WALL OF BITTERNESS

One of the ways that God broke down my walls was through a Bible study called How to Be Free from Bitterness. For the past two years, I've been in a Bible study with two other women. We studied the last part of Romans, Titus, and Joshua through Precept Ministries International. At the completion of the Joshua study, one of the ladies in the group suggested bitterness as our next focus.

I thought, "Okay, I'm sure there is something that I can learn," but I felt some skepticism about it.

Let all bitterness, and wrath, and anger, and clamor, and evil speaking, be put away from you, with all malice.

—Ephesians 4:31

Our study of bitterness helped to sand down some of the roughness in my heart towards my father. We studied and discussed how to be free from bitterness, how to forgive others anger and rage, how to restrain the tongue, and how to quit looking to the self for answers. I read. I wrote. I prayed. I shared at group time. I flowed—until we hit the part about bitterness towards parents. My defenses flew up.

"Do I really have to talk about my father again? I thought I was over that. I am sick of thinking and talking about him. He is human, not going to be perfect. I want him out of my story," I thought.

The study showed me that I had more work to do: I had to give all my hurt around my father to the Father, and I had to give all the hurt I suffered from his wife to the Father and then—get this—I had to honor them and really mean it. It could not be my lips saying one thing and my heart saying another. My lips and heart had to speak the same message. It was a process.

"Honor your father and mother and your days will be long."

So this is what I arrived at, in my mind and heart, to reach that place where I'm honoring them: my mother and father are part of the hurt in my life, but they are also part of the strength in my life.

I thank them for giving me life. My father and mother both came from circumstances that were tough for them. My father's mother gave birth to him when she was just 17 years old. She moved from her hometown and left my father with her parents. My mother grew up in a house with her mother and stepfather. She never knew her biological father. She knew his name and occupation, but nothing else. She has longed to find him, but at this point she is resigned to that fact that he is most likely deceased (my mother is 69 years old), and she will never know that part of her lineage. Both of my parents have their own stories of rejection, so I understand how they could treat me the way they did, and, at the same time, I acknowledge that some of the decisions that they made deeply impacted me.

CRACKING BITTERNESS THROUGH FORGIVENESS

First, I called my father. I did not talk about anything deep. I dipped my feet in the shallow end of the pool—small talk and niceties.

Then the Lord had me send a letter to both my father and his wife, my stepmother. I could not ignore my father's wife anymore because I love the Lord and the Lord says to honor your father and mother and that husband and wife are one. If I was to honor my father, I had to honor his wife because she is a part of him.

I did it. I sent the letter.

My father called me. He did not understand why I was asking for his forgiveness. But I understood. I had been disrespectful toward him and his wife during my younger years, and even if they may have deserved it, that was not for me to do. God said that I was to honor my father's position, not how he necessarily did his job. And I had to get that wickedness out of my heart.

So, even though my father did not comprehend my reason for asking for his forgiveness, he forgave me and he said that he loved me.

At the time, it did not register that he'd really said he loved me. I brushed over it quickly. However, my father saying he loved me was HUGE. I did not let it register at the time because I had, up until that point, experienced his actions as unloving. Nevertheless, I've realized that I must accept his words, so my heart will soften in that hardened area . . . *CRACK . . .*

THE WALL OF NEGATIVE THOUGHT PATHWAYS

In Romans 12:1–2, the Word of God says:

*Therefore I urge you, brethren, by the mercies of God, to present your bodies, a living and holy sacrifice, acceptable to God, which is your spiritual service of worship. And do not be conformed to this world, but **be transformed by the renewing of your mind**, so that you may prove what the will of God is, that which is good and acceptable and perfect. [words bolded by author]*

My mind needs to be continually renewed, and the Word of God is the only way to renew my mind. From a Pastor at our church I learned about Dr. Caroline Leaf, a neuroscientist who is a follower of Christ.

Through scientific findings Dr. Leaf supports what God says in His Word about our minds needing to be renewed. She says science is finally catching up with what God has already said about our minds. Dr. Leaf developed a 21-day brain detox program that helps to bring about the renewal that our minds so desperately need.

Dr. Leaf explains that negative thoughts build strong neurological connections in our minds the more we focus on them. These negative thoughts direct other thoughts and behaviors.

God has designed our minds so that we can look at these negative thoughts, capture them, and change them; therefore, by changing the direction of our thoughts, we can change the direction of our lives.

The Word of God says to "take every thought captive to the obedience of Christ" (2 Corinthians 10:5), and that is exactly what Dr. Leaf's brain detox program helped me to do.

Before starting the 21-day program, Dr. Leaf asks you to pray and ask the Holy Spirit to show you the one thought that you need to start with. In doing this, as I prayed, the Holy Spirit told me that I needed to kill the toxic thought, "A specific close family member does not really love me." When I felt it in my inner man, I knew it was definitely an area that I needed to confront.

With an illustration, Dr. Leaf shows that thoughts, negative or positive, true or false, make connections in our brain. The illustration shows how toxic thoughts form all these black branches in the brain. Dr. Leaf promises that the one thought that the Holy Spirit shows you that you need to change will become nontoxic and grow healthy branches in the brain over the 21 days of the detox program.

Briefly, the 21-day detox consists of five main steps that I participated in daily:

1. Gathering
2. Focused Reflection
3. Journal
4. Revisit
5. Active Reach

    (For a more detailed explanations of these steps, check out 21daybraindetox.com.)

CRACKING THAT ONE THOUGHT WITH THE 21-DAY DETOX

To get a clearer picture of how I used the program, here is the work from day 15. I began with watching a video of Dr. Caroline Leaf. The focus of the video was finding a balance between sin awareness (admit it, quit it, and beat it) and grace awareness (choose to apply the Blood of Jesus; God forgives and cleanses). After the video, I praised the Lord for being Who He is. After worship, I began to gather awareness of my thoughts (step 1). Then I highlighted a thought that stood out in my thinking (step 2). I journaled about that thought (step 3). The completion of the journaling section brought me to the revisit step (step 4) in which I journaled the following:

I am not trusting God. My faith is in me. I need to focus on trusting God for all things—not just the big, but the small. Trust in the Lord with all my heart.

In the active reach step (step 5), my plan for the rest of day 15 was to state Proverbs 3:5–7, seven times out loud throughout the day:

Trust in the Lord with all your heart,
And lean not on your own understanding;
In all your ways acknowledge Him,
And He shall direct [a] your paths. Do not be wise in your own eyes;
Fear the Lord and depart from evil. (New King James Version)

This plan was more thorough than just reading a Scripture in the morning, closing the Bible, and never revisiting what I read for the rest of the day. It's like the difference between a surface clean and a deep clean. If you have not mopped your floors in months, one little spray of floor cleaner is not going to clean them. That job requires getting on your hands and knees and scrubbing with lots of muscle. The negative thought—that that close family member did not really love me—had been in my mind for years. YEARS, not months. I needed more than just one little spray to remove it from my mind to clean it out. Reading Proverbs 3:5–7 throughout the day was my way of SCRUBBING (with muscle) that old thought out and reminding me that a new thought had penetrated into my mind.

The brain detox really washed my mind and scrubbed it down with the Word of God, and God's Word reinforced the real truth. At the end of 21 days, through Scripture, focus, and practice, my mind had been renewed. The process pulled immense energy from me. It took a great amount of energy to concentrate on what was running through my mind constantly. Through the brain detox program, thoughts not of God were not allowed to run freely through my mind. I learned to take the thought captive into the obedience of Christ.

Casting down imaginations, and every high thing that exalteth itself against the knowledge of God, and bringing into captivity every thought to the obedience of Christ.

—2 Corinthians 10:5 (KJV)

During those 21 days, some days felt like I was walking a mile in 12 inches of snow. Heaviness. Exhaustion. I have yet to complete my second cycle of 21 days. God's strength is the only way that I will complete a second cycle (21 more days with a new thought and reinforcing the work completed with the first thought). Nevertheless, the wall is being broken . . . *CRACK* . . .

THE WALL OF SHAME AND BLAME

Another way that God broke down the wall of defense in my road to healing is the Bible study called Binding Up the Brokenhearted offered through Healing Hearts Ministry (healinghearts. org). This pivotal study intensified my healing process. I would STRONGLY, HIGHLY recommend this study to anyone who has had an abortion and wants to heal fully in the name of Jesus Christ of Nazareth. The study covers many areas of your life so that no area is kept from God as He heals you. Uncovering and exploring all those areas was effective in setting me free.

Forgiveness is the area of the study that I will share.

For this is My blood of the covenant, which is poured out for many for forgiveness of sins.

—Matthew 26:28

And their sins and their lawless deeds I will remember no more. Now where there is forgiveness of these things, there is no longer any offer for sins.

—Hebrews 10:17–18

When I thought of forgiveness in relationship to me aborting my babies, the first person whom I thought required forgiveness was myself. Once the wall of denial began to crumble and I acknowledged that I had done something wrong in the sight of God, I desperately wanted the Lord's forgiveness.

In the Scriptures noted above, it is clear that Jesus Christ forgives and His Blood covers the sin once and for all. So, I did not have to keep going back to Him over and over and over again asking Him to forgive that I aborted my three children. But, I felt like I had to. Did this mean I had to forgive myself?

The Bible does not state that we must forgive ourselves for sins. There is only One who can forgive sin and that is God—Father, Son, and Holy Spirit. So, I learned that I did not have to forgive myself; what I had to do was keep giving the thought "I am still guilty even though I am a child of God" over to God. To this day, I continue to give that thought to God whenever it pops into my head. Because the truth is—I am forgiven.

CRACKING THE BLAME AND SHAME

In Ezra 9:5–8 (Amplified), Ezra writes, through the inspiration of the Holy Spirit:

At the evening offering I arose from my [time of] humiliation and penitence and having torn my clothing and my robe, I fell on my knees and stretched out my hands to the Lord my God, and I said, "O my God, I am ashamed and embarrassed to lift up my face to You, my God, for our wrongdoings have risen higher than our heads and our guilt has grown to the heavens. Since the days of our fathers to this day we have been exceedingly guilty; and on account of our wrongdoings we, our kings, and our priests have been handed over to the kings of the lands, to the sword, to captivity, to plundering, and to complete shame, as it is today. But now for a brief moment grace has been [shown to us] from the Lord our God, who has left us a surviving remnant and has given us a peg (secure hold) in His holy place, that our God may enlighten our eyes and give us a little reviving in our bondage.

I felt the anguish that Ezra described as I prayed to the Lord Jesus Christ about my three abortions—my three babies. Sorrow and guilt and shame surrounded me.

After reading Ezra 9:5–8, one of the tasks in Binding Up the Brokenhearted was to write a prayer to the Lord expressing any feelings of guilt and shame. I wrote this:

Dear Heavenly Father, Jesus Christ, my Savior, and Holy Spirit,

I thank You for being who You are—mighty, holy, merciful, full of grace, just, and LOVE.

Thank You for forgiving me for my many sins—including the sin of murder and fornication. I felt that I had dropped all of my shame until I encountered the question on the doctor's office form. Lord, I ask that You help me to be honest about my past abortions to whomever You want me to share.

I pray that I will always have compassion for the babies that I murdered. I also pray that I will no longer hold onto the guilt and the

*shame, but that I will give that to You with a repenting heart and an
open heart to use me the way that You choose in regard to sharing
the truth about my sin and the truth about Your grace and mercy
regarding all of our sins. I also pray that You deliver me from any pride
that I have around this issue.*

I love You.

In the name of Jesus Christ of Nazareth.

. . . *CRACK* . . .

Besides asking God for forgiveness for myself, forgiving the fathers of the babies that I aborted was also in order. In Matthew 6:12, the Word of the Lord says, "And forgive our debts, as we also have forgiven our debtors." Matthew 6:14 goes onto say, "For if you forgive others for their transgressions, Your heavenly Father will also forgive you." I had heard these Scriptures before. I had memorized the Lord's Prayer when I was a little girl. But in application—what did these Scriptures mean?

Because these two Scriptures on forgiveness were written in Greek way before they were translated into English, I looked up the Greek word for "forgive," which is aphiemi. It is a verb—an action. The definition for aphiemi is "to send away, to send forth, yield up, to expire, to let go, let alone, let be, disregard, to leave, to not discuss."

In the beginning of my walk with Christ, I used to say that when I forgave someone, it did not mean that we would then be best buddies and go out to tea; instead it entailed a true letting go that occurred inside of me. According to Ken Sande and Kevin Johnson from the book, *The Peacemaker,* solid forgiveness requires that you do not rehearse the wrong over and over in your mind, nor do you discuss it with other people. You must let go of the offense.

I had to let go of the prison in which I had placed each one of these men (young men at the time).

Father #1—I thought he loved me. Not only did he not love me, he was not there for me and he replaced me with another woman within months. His crime (in my eyes): *deception.*

Father #2—He did not believe that I was pregnant. When I asked for his financial contribution towards the abortion, he said I was lying about the pregnancy to secure money from him. He also said IF I was pregnant, he was not the father. His crime (in my eyes): *insensitivity.*

Father #3—He did not persuade me to believe that he truly did not believe in abortion AND that he would be there for the child and me. His crime (in my eyes): *lack of conviction and commitment.*

Nevertheless, I had to forgive them—that is, no longer hold them in my heart with contempt. I had to let go of the disappointment. I had to let go of how I thought they should have handled the situation. I had . . . to . . . let . . . go. I had to yield up those feelings. I had to cast that care onto the Lord. During the Binding Up the Brokenhearted Bible study, I said a prayer to release all of them. As I have been writing this book, I have prayed that God bless them . . . *CRACK* . . .

I have found that it helps to pray for those you do not like. Prayers disarm the hate and venom. I write this as if it is easy to do. For me, at this point, it has been easy to do, and that may be because of the process that God has been taking me through up to this point. If you would have asked me if I had hard feelings toward any of these men, just four years ago, I may have spit on the ground to show the intensity of my disgust. But I do not feel that now. And I thank God for that.

THE WALL OF IGNORANCE

During our Christian walk, the Lord may show us thoughts or deeds that He needs to change, not as a judgment that we are "bad," but rather as a call to clean out what separates us from the blessing and work He has for us. And sometimes these thoughts and deeds may not even be areas that we have considered.

If we had forgotten the name of our God,
Or extended our hands to a strange god,
Would not God find this out?
For He knows the secrets of the heart.

—Psalm 44:20–21 (NASB)

The Binding Up the Brokenhearted study confronted an area that I was not expecting: examining involvement with cults, the occult, and other religions. As part of the study, I had to repent of several activities from my past. The following were included as ungodly activities: dowsing, horoscopes, horror movies/books, reincarnation, and yoga.

I declared out loud that I no longer wanted any association with these activities, and I repented.

Why would some of these be areas that the Lord wants me to address and surrender to Him? And what does it mean to repent?

BREAKING THE IGNORANCE
THROUGH REPENTANCE

Back to the analogy of the car from chapter 2: have you ever taken your car to the service department to fix one problem and they find problems you were unaware even existed? That's what this was like for me. I was unaware that these past activities affected my life, but my lack of knowledge—ignorance—did not mean that the areas did not have to be repaired.

Taking a closer look at the Scripture 1 John 1:8 and of the word "repent" shed some light as how God was using this in my healing. The Scripture 1 John 1:8–10 (KJV) states:

> *If we say we have no sin, we deceive ourselves, and the truth is not in us. If we confess our sins, He is faithful and just to forgive us our sins and to cleanse us from all unrighteousness. If we say we have not sinned, we make him a liar, and his word is not in us.*

According to David Guzik, pastor and renown commentator on the Bible, this Scripture explains the reason we, as believers, still must confess when we do things that do not align with God's way. Through the confession, first, and repentance, second, we are cleansed and remain in fellowship with God.

Another pastor once explained it like this: imagine that you have an empty paper towel tube and that tube is the communication line between you and God. When we have wrongs in our life that we are unaware of and that the Lord brings to our attention, if we do not confess them and repent, these wrongs clog up the tube, hence, clogging up our communication with God. For the believer, the confession and repentance unclogs the tube.

What does it mean to repent? The Greek word for repent, meta-noeo, means "to change one's mind; to change one's mind for better, heartily to amend with abhorrence of one's past sins." In her book, *The Power of the Praying Woman,* Stormie Omartian defines repentance as "to change your mind. To turn and walk the other way. Repentance means being deeply sorry for what you have done that you will do whatever it takes to keep it from happening again."

This section in the Binding Up the Brokenhearted study was there for me to become mindful that there may be areas in my life that I am unaware of that are blocking my connection to God. And I have to be open to listening to God, always asking Him to show me and give me a willingness to (1) confess the thought or deed as wrong; and (2) repent.

As I said at the start of this subsection, these activities would not have come to my mind as things to repair, but once they were brought to my attention, I prayed about them, and I perceived that I needed to confess and repent. And that is what I did. I confessed and I spoke a prayer of repentance . . . *CRACK* . . .

IN SUMMARY

As part of the repair of my abortion wounds and preparation for sharing how He healed me, the Lord cracked several walls that had been erected in my life—walls that impeded my restoration: the walls of bitterness, negative thoughts, shame and blame, and ignorance. The demolition of these walls did not happen overnight. What I described for you happened over two years. I experienced discomfort and pain. And the process is ongoing. Nevertheless, all has been worth it because it has led me to God's peace where I know that I am truly forgiven for aborting my children. And little did I know, God was preparing me to face the biggest truth surrounding my abortions, a truth that I had denied for 30 years . . .

INVITATION TO PONDER

For hope and healing, ponder these Scriptures:

- Ephesians 4:31–32
- Ephesians 5:26
- Romans 12:2
- 2 Corinthians 10:5
- Matthew 26:28
- Matthew 6:14
- 1 John 1:8–10

Also, consider the following:

- What walls have you erected in your life?
- Pray and ask the Holy Spirit to show you your walls. And ask Him to give you the courage to face them. Ask Him to destroy them.

MY WALLS

_____
_____
_____
_____
_____
_____
_____
_____
_____
_____
_____
_____
_____
_____
_____
_____
_____
_____
_____
_____
_____
_____
_____
_____
_____

_____
_____
_____
_____
_____
_____
_____
_____
_____
_____
_____
_____
_____
_____
_____
_____
_____
_____
_____
_____
_____
_____
_____
_____
_____
_____

Chapter 7

BRINGING THE TRUTH TO LIGHT

One of the lies that I believed during my 30-year period of silence about my abortions was—*I did not kill babies. The abortions had only been medical procedures that removed tissue that stood in the way of my future.* God began to show me that that idea, to which I held tightly, was, indeed, a lie. It was not true.

WHICH WAS WHICH?

Because I was a board member of the Lifecare Center, a pregnancy crisis center, our community outreach director asked me to volunteer to serve at the center's booth at the county fair. LifeCare shared the booth with several other pro-life organizations active in the county. I agreed to staff the booth and share our mission with others in the community.

As part of our table setup, we displayed clay and plastic models of babies at each stage of development from conception to birth. We also had these pins of little feet that showed what a baby's feet looked like at 10 weeks. Seeing the baby's development stages in models that I could touch and feel and seeing the pin of the little feet exploded that lie for me.

This new information could not fit into the thoughts that I'd previously had. One had to be truth, and one had to be a lie.

But—which was which?

According to *cold, hard evidence-based biological findings*—the models were developed based on science. The little feet depicted on the pin were based on scientific findings—what then did it mean for me to accept this truth?

It meant that I'd permitted three of my babies to be killed.

—OR—

According to *friends who'd had abortions and the clinic staff that performed the abortions on me*—what did it mean to accept these sources as truth?

It meant that I'd permitted tissue to be extracted from my body, like getting a tooth pulled.

I had to decide what I was going to believe.

Because God had already been moving in my life so that I could be free, totally, from this sin—so my house could be swept clean (Luke 11:24–25)—I fully recognized which one I had to believe. I was not going to hold onto the tissue lie because, according to the Word of God, Satan is the father of lies and Jesus Christ is truth and grace—and truth sets me free.

Truth—there were three babies inside of me, and I allowed all three of them to be killed.

THE BIBLE ON ABORTION

Binding the Brokenhearted Bible study also contributed to the exposure of the truth.

There was a section in the study that showed the developmental stages of a baby starting with the first 24 hours after conception on up to 20 weeks after conception. After that, we examined how God sees abortion. Here is some of what we discovered from the Bible: God considered babies killed by fire as sacrifices to false gods to be abominations (Deuteronomy 18:10–12). He also hates the shedding of innocent blood (Proverbs 6:16–19).

In my small-group Bible study, we studied the book of Joshua. In Joshua we read how God had commanded people to provide a place of refuge for those who murdered by accident, but to let the avengers of blood kill anyone who murdered with hate in their hearts and/or with intent to kill.

What this Joshua passage meant in terms of me: because I consented to the abortions with intent to kill, even though I had not considered it murder at the time, under God's law, I could have been killed as punishment.

After reading this passage in Joshua, I was humbled and thanked God for His grace and mercy.

God brought revelation in His Word about my abortions, and I had to accept it. Otherwise, I would be swallowed up by the lie and the shame and the guilt. I did not want that.

LIES ABOUT ABORTION

The lie that I believed—*that babies in the womb were not human, just tissue, unwanted tissue that can be thrown away*—is perpetuated and upheld in our culture. I am not absolving myself of responsibility. Nevertheless, it is important to know that there are many messages in society that promote abortion and abortion-mindedness. The lie comes from many sources—both internally and externally. And these deceitful messages contribute to the acceptance and encouragement of the practice.

Recently at a chiropractor's office I picked up *Ebony*, a magazine that John Johnson established in 1945 to focus on black American life. *Ebony* has been a staple in the black community for 71 years. The issue I picked up focused on family—it was actually called "The Family Issue." It included articles about blended families, the cultural impact of our first family—the Obamas—and the legacy of *The Cosby Show* in the midst of the sexual misconduct allegations against Bill Cosby.

Nestled inside this issue was an article that caught my eye, an article titled "Choice under Fire." In this article, the author gathered data from several resources that justified a woman having an abortion. Some of the reasons listed to justify an abortion were that she could die in childbirth, that her community may not provide her access to quality education, healthcare, and safe neighborhoods, and that economically she could not afford to take care of the child. All are real problems in some communities, but do they justify homicide?

If I read the morning paper and saw that a mother murdered three children, ages 10, 6, and 1, because the public schools in her area were terrible and the gang violence was climbing daily, what would I think? Would I say, "Oh, the law should excuse her?"

If I learned that a college girl murdered a five-year-old that she was babysitting because the little girl distracted her from finishing her homework, thus hindered her ability to graduate and find a good-paying job, would that be acceptable? The truth is no matter the statistics or reasons, murder is murder—despite what the media tells us. TRUTH.

According to the Abortion Index,[4] between 1967 and June 2016, 59,400,000 babies have been aborted in the United States. The number of Americans of ALL ages and races murdered daily by handguns is 28. The number of American babies of ALL races killed every day by abortion is 3,000. That means for every one person killed by a handgun, 107 people are killed by an abortion. TRUTH.

PRODUCT OF TRUTH

After understanding and accepting and soaking in truth, the Lord prompted me to name my babies. He put in my spirit to name them so that I could acknowledge that they were real people—just as real as the three sons that I did allow to live and gave birth to. He guided me through this step using one of my friends who is a born-again follower of Jesus Christ and who allows the Holy Spirit to order her steps.

My friend, Lisa, shared with me that her sister had had a miscarriage, and a counselor recommended to her sister, as part of her stages of grief, that she name the baby. Lisa said that she knew that my situation was different in that I had not had miscarriages, yet what was the same for her sister and me was a baby's life had ended.

I pondered that for a while—and the guilt began to rise up: "If I named the babies, that would mean that they really were people that did not make it here to this earth because of me. It will never be known what they could have contributed because I made the decision that they could not come here." That was a heavy load.

After the acceptance of the truth that I'd killed my babies, the heaviness pushed me to the next action: I had to grieve. I had to cry for them. I needed to cry for them. I needed to let my heart break for them. I had never ever cried about aborting my children because, as I said earlier, I hadn't considered them children. The abortions seemed necessary, so I could "get the most out of my life." So, crying for them had never entered my mind or heart.

But, as the Lord Jesus Christ had been breaking down my walls of defense and denial, my heart could finally feel for those babies— my babies.

I walked into my prayer closet. I knelt down with my prayer blanket over my head and asked the Lord to forgive me for murdering my babies. I felt the sting of that truth—and the missed lives— and I cried. I finally cried . . . after 30 years.

I felt the hurt and the sorrow and the regret and the missing of the love I could have received from them and the love I could have given to them. And what I would have taught them and what I would have learned from them. And how my boys, who are living, would have loved them. How my family would have been so different. I cried. Thirty years of denial let go on the floor of my closet.

In order to name the babies, I asked God to tell me their genders and to give me their names. This is what God told me: for the first baby, his name is Stephen. For the second baby, her name is Nicole. And the third baby, his name is Alexander. If you know the names of my living children, you would know that I would have never chosen these names. These names are much simpler than names of my taste. So without a shadow of doubt, I am clear that God gave me these names.

All of the names are derived from Greek words. Stephen means "wreath, crown, honor and/or reward." Nicole means "people's victory." And Alexander means "defender of men." The meanings fascinated me. God had chosen very strong names for each of my babies.

I asked the Lord to please tell Stephen, Nicole, and Alexander for me that I deeply regretted terminating their lives, that I wanted them to forgive me, and that I loved them. I asked for their forgiveness many times after that in prayer.

Now I know my heart was being softened toward them each time I acknowledged them.

Releasing the hardness in my heart has opened me up to be more loving to other people who are close to me.

CONTINUED SURRENDER

I hadn't realized how keeping my heart hard toward my own flesh and blood—Stephen, Nicole, and Alexander—was keeping me from loving people right in front of me. I do not know if my family would say that I have softened, but this old heart—already new from Christ—is even fresher because of the love I have for my babies and the love I've expressed for my babies. I would have never thought that by being so cold toward Stephen, Nicole, and Alexander that I was not experiencing the new level that Christ had for me.

On the day of my salvation, I surrendered all to Christ—all that I was aware of. And, now, 13 years later, I surrender my wounds of abortion to the Savior Jesus Christ. This process that God has taken me through is explained by the theologians and backed up by Scripture as "progressive sanctification,"[5] where the word "sanctification" means "an act of being set apart to a sacred purpose or religious use; freed from sin: purification."

When I initially put my trust in Jesus Christ, when I said yes to His plan of salvation (see Romans 10:9–10), He immediately declared me saved, holy, and righteous—a new creature—in Jesus Christ (Romans 3:22; 2 Corinthians 5:17; Ephesians 2:4—6). Theologians call this "positional" or "definitive sanctification."

The moment I said yes, I was definitely saved. After that point, comes the progressive sanctification. This is the journey on which we walk with the Father, Son, and Holy Spirit to make us more like the Son (2 Corinthians 3:18; Ephesians 4:23–24). This process continues to the end of our earthly life. The healing of the abortion wounds was one mark in my progressive sanctification. There will be other marks. As Pastor W. Duncan Rankin wrote in his article "Being and Becoming,"[6] "We, by God's grace, must continue the journey of sanctification day by day. In addition to being called holy, Christians are also becoming holy."

I am learning that I surrendered to Christ, and I must continually surrender to Christ, to not take on the weight of past, present, and future wrongs. I am reminded of the profound words of an old hymn, "I Surrender All":

All to Jesus I surrender,
All to Him I freely give;
I will ever love and trust Him,
In His presence daily live.

I surrender all,
I surrender all;
All to Thee, my blessed Savior,
I surrender all.

All to Jesus I surrender,
Humbly at His feet I bow;
Worldly pleasures all forsaken,
Take me, Jesus, take me now.

All to Jesus I surrender,
Make me, Savior, wholly Thine;
Let me feel the Holy Spirit,
Truly know that Thou art mine.
All to Jesus I surrender,
Lord, I give myself to Thee;
Fill me with Thy love and power,
Let Thy blessing fall on me.

All to Jesus I surrender,
Now I feel the sacred flame;
Oh, the joy of full salvation!
Glory, glory, to His Name!

—Judson W. Van DeVenter, 1896

GUILTY NO MORE—A DEEP DIVE INTO CHRIST'S SACRIFICE

Another lie that God has been exposing is the lie that I have to hold onto guilt for the rest of my life because I terminated the lives of three of my children. In fact—I am forgiven. TRUTH.

Currently, our small group is studying the Book of Hebrews. This is such an appropriate Book of the Bible to study when you have lingering guilt about past sins. The Book of Hebrews explains in-depth how we have a great High Priest in heaven, Jesus Christ, who continually intercedes for those who have given their lives to Him. That is, Christ is the High Priest for those who have spoken that He is Lord of their lives.

What does that mean for Christ to be your High Priest?

In Hebrews 9, the author, through inspiration of the Holy Spirit, talks about the first covenant (the Law) and compares it to the new covenant (Grace and Truth through Christ). The rituals that took place in the tabernacle to cleanse the high priest and the people from sin are briefly described. To gain a full picture of these rituals, we reviewed Leviticus 16 in our Bible study. Such a beautiful picture is painted in Leviticus 16 of the Day of Atonement.

The Day of Atonement was the one time of year that the high priest, and the high priest only, was allowed to go into the Holy of Holies, behind the second veil in the tent of meeting, to repent for his sins and the sins of the people. The Lord required the high priest to implement elaborate steps to cover the sins committed in ignorance.

The high priest could not just walk in and say a simple prayer and leave. He had to wear special clothes, he had to wash, he had to bring incense, he had to take blood from a bull for himself and blood from a goat for the people. He laid hands on a second goat—the scapegoat—which was symbolic of him placing all of the sins of the people upon the goat. Then, he sent the goat out into the wilderness with all the sins. A man from the community was assigned to take the goat out into the wilderness. This man had to be cleansed also when he returned.

I am giving you the short version of what took place. I highly recommend that you read Leviticus 16 in several versions, so you can see the detail, care, and holiness that surrounded the high priest going to God on behalf of himself and the people to ask for forgiveness and cleansing of all their sins. Leviticus 16 clearly highlights the seriousness of sin and being cleansed from it.

After attaining a more vivid picture of what the Old Testament high priest did in the tabernacle, I returned to Hebrews 9 to better understand the significance of Christ's sacrifice for our sins.

In the Old Testament, the high priest had to make the sacrifice of the blood from the bull and the goat once a year.

Christ sacrificed His blood once for all.

The Old Testament sacrifices could not take away our sin. Those sacrifices just reminded us of our sin and how merciful God was to allow us to be cleansed so that He could commune with us. Nevertheless, "the blood of bulls and goats could never perfect us—take away our sin forever and forever." The Word of God says in Hebrews 9 that without blood, sins cannot be forgiven. So the blood was necessary, but it could not fully cleanse. Consequently, the high priest had to continue to enter the temple, the Holy of Holies, year after year.

But God brings Christ to the scene. And He becomes our High Priest and our perfect sacrifice, so that our sins are taken away forever (Hebrews 9:26). Forever.

It is only with the blood of Christ that our sins are forgiven. Forever.

It is not over time that our sins are forgiven—the saying, "Time heals all wounds"—it's not so.

It is not through doing good deeds that our sins are forgiven. Somewhere inside of me because I encouraged abortion-minded friends to keep their babies (this was after I began to follow Christ), I thought I was making up for the abortions that I'd had. Not so.

It is only with blood—the blood of Jesus Christ—that our sins are forgiven once and for all. FORGIVEN FOREVER.

When I was holding onto the sin of my abortion, keeping it secret and keeping the shame and guilt, I was saying that Christ's sacrifice on the cross was not enough to cleanse me. I thought my sin was BIGGER than Christ's sacrifice. I did not consciously say that, but the knots in my stomach when someone would mention abortion said that. It is only by remembering that Christ paid that price that I am able to keep my mind from falling back into guilt and shame.

I am free. I am forgiven. TRUTH.

READY TO SERVE?

One of the Scriptures that the Lord just had me recently memorize is Hebrews 4:14–16 (KJV):

Seeing then that we have a great High Priest that has passed into the heavens, Jesus, Son of God, let us hold fast our profession. For we have not an high priest that can not be touched by the feeling of our infirmities, but like as we are tempted in all points yet without sin. Let us therefore come boldly to the throne of grace to obtain mercy and to find grace to help in time of need.

I have a High Priest—you have a High Priest (if you are a follower of Christ)—to whom we can take everything and from whom we can obtain mercy and grace. We can take these thoughts to Him, and He restores. And if it takes time, we can go to Him repeatedly. We can go to other believers and ask for prayer. We are not in this alone, and we are not in His kingdom without a purpose. We are to glorify Him, and we are to serve the living God.

For some women, their past sin of abortion has stopped them from serving whole-heartedly. And when I say, "serve," I do not just mean serving in church. I mean serving with your life, being obedient to whatever God has called you to do, and moving from being stuck to being obedient and being used by God.

Serving can take on many forms. Your serving may mean loving your family more fully. It may mean letting go of all bitterness and wrath (Ephesians 4:32). I do not know what the area is in your life that has been poisoned by holding onto the guilt and shame of an abortion.

I just know that for those who are truly ready to walk in the newness of Christ, this is the hour to do it and let go.

In church recently one of our pastors preached and taught about our intent and purpose being in Christ, and how some people were allowing their past to strangle their future: "Some are still making what was, what IS today." In arguing that once we are in Christ, our past can no longer control our future, he brought up the story of the Apostle Paul.

The Apostle Paul, himself, tells us that in his past he was responsible for the death of some Christians, "When the blood of your martyr Stephen was shed, I stood there giving my approval" (Acts 22:20, NIV).

However, Paul was transformed on the road to Damascus (it should be noted that he went by Saul and only changed his name to Paul after the transformation):

As he was traveling, it happened that he was approaching Damascus, and suddenly a light from heaven flashed around him; and he fell to the ground and heard a voice saying to him, 'Saul, Saul, why are you persecuting Me?' And he said, 'Who are You, Lord? And He said, "I am Jesus whom you are persecuting, but get up and enter the city, and it will be told you what you must do."

—Act 9:3-6

From this encounter with Christ, Saul/Paul was left blind for three days, and he did not eat or drink for those three days.

Next, Christ sent a disciple named Ananias to Saul/Paul to give him back his sight and his mission:

But the Lord said to him, 'Go, for he is a chosen instrument of Mine,
to bear My name before the Gentiles and kings and the sons of Israel;
for I will show him how much he must suffer for My name's sake.'

—Acts 9:15–16)

Christ had a mission for Saul/Paul, so Paul had to forget his past as Saul and move forward. Paul explains this in Philippians 3:13–14:

Brethren, I do not regard myself as having laid hold of it yet; but one
thing I do: forgetting what lies behind and reaching forward to what
lies ahead, I press on toward the goal for the prize of the upward
call of God in Christ Jesus.

The Greek word for "forget" is *epilanthanomai*, a verb that means "to forget, neglecting, no longer caring for, forgotten, given over to oblivion, uncared for."

The Greek word for "reaching" is *epekteinomai*, also a verb. It means "to stretch out to or towards, to stretch (one's self) forward to."

The Greek word for "press" is *dioko*. It is a verb that means "to run swiftly in order to catch a person or thing, to run after; to press on, figuratively of one who in a race runs swiftly to reach the goal; metaphorically, to seek after eagerly, earnestly; endeavor to acquire."

(1) We must FORGET, meaning we must no longer spend time in our head mulling over past sin. Or for those of us who had an abortion and thought that it was no big deal, we must no longer mull over that lie that allows us to justify our sin.

(2) We must REACH, meaning stretch ourselves forward to the future without the past defining that future.

(3) And we must PRESS, meaning pursue passionately, earnestly, eagerly what God has called us to do as if we did not have forever to do it, but a short amount of time.

Just as we must do, Paul did—FORGET, REACH, and PRESS.

Scholars agree that Paul penned eight Books in the New Testament (some say 14). He *forgot* his past and *reached* and *pressed* into what he was called to do—challenges and all—he did what God called him to do. And we are the benefactors of his obedience.

Someone in the kingdom or in the world is waiting for you. God has designed you with a uniqueness, and only you can bring to this world that gift and/or talent. I pray you walk in the newness of Christ.

IN SUMMARY

The title of this chapter is Bringing the Truth to Light. As the Lord carefully attended my wounds, He showed me the main lie that had had kept me from asking for forgiveness regarding the abortions. The lie He showed me was—*the babies were not babies, but tissue.* Exposure of this grand lie permitted me to acknowledge the lives of my babies by naming them and full asking for God's forgiveness. In turn, the massive weight of guilt was released from me. I feel free to tell my story, and I feel free to serve the Lord whole-heartedly because the truth was brought to light and to the Light—Jesus Christ.

Christ is the Light of the World. Whoever follows Him will not walk in Darkness (John 8:12). I invite you to give the darkness of your abortion to Him. Give your life to Him. Do you know Him? If not, the next chapter will show you how to declare Jesus Christ as the Lord of your life and your Savior.

INVITATION TO PONDER

For hope and healing, ponder these Scriptures:

- Leviticus 16
- John 8:31—32
- Ephesians 4:23–24
- Hebrews 4:14–16
- Hebrews 9:26

Also, consider the following:

- Have you acknowledged that in your consenting to an abortion you took the life of your unborn child?
- How have you honored your child?
- How have you grieved for your child?
- Have you surrendered your action of consenting to an abortion over to the Lord?

MY REFLECTIONS

_____

_____

_____

_____

_____

_____

_____

_____

_____

_____

_____

_____

_____

_____

_____

_____

_____

_____

_____

_____

_____

_____

_____

_____

_____

_____

_____

Chapter 8

GIVE IT OVER AND JOIN THE KINGDOM

The wounds surrounding abortion are real. The wounds present before an abortion are what make the abortion the "solution" to an unwanted to pregnancy.

In my case, my father being absent was a great wound and my inability to forgive him deepened that wound. These deep wounds brought me to choosing abortion as my "solution" to the unwanted pregnancies, a solution, which in turn wounded me even more on the physical, emotional, and symbolic levels.

God walked, and is walking, me through the healing of these wounds. Sharing with you my story is one way in which my healing is taking place. Your reading my story and taking inspiration and strength from it to start (or continue) your healing journey is another way for me to heal.

While your story and circumstances may be quite different from mine, what is true for both of us is—God is faithful to heal if we give it to Him.

The Lord will order your steps in how He will choose to repair your wounds.

If you do not know Jesus Christ as your Lord and Savior, I pray that you give your life to Him. It is simple to give your life to the Lord. You pray—that is, speak to the Lord—and say to Him that Jesus Christ is Lord and that you believe in your heart that God raised Jesus from the dead. Also express your sorrow for not walking with Him, repent, and purpose to turn away from ways that are not the ways of God. And finally find a Bible-teaching church, so you may grow in the Lord Jesus Christ.

I pray that my story has encouraged you to acknowledge your pain and give it over to God. Throw off the shame that Satan has put on you and see that God is truly glorified when we tell the truth. In the truth, we proclaim the goodness of God. We lift Him up. And when we lift Him up, more people will be drawn to Him and join the kingdom of God.

MY REFLECTIONS

_____

_____

_____

_____

_____

_____

_____

_____

_____

_____

_____

_____

_____

Epilogue

I learned in a sermon that Paul, from the New Testament, changed his own name from Saul to Paul. Saul was a very respected Hebrew name. It represented stature; whereas Paul, at the time, was a common Roman (Gentile) name. Paul changed his name to reflect his mission given to him by God. That is, God gave Paul the job of sharing the good news of Jesus Christ with the Gentiles. The Gentiles were Paul's mission field.

At the beginning of my walk with God, when I first truly surrendered my life to God, I had a dream in which God named me Tabitha. I woke up frightened because my only reference to Tabitha was the little girl on the television show Bewitched, and Tabitha was a little witch.

Later, I was directed to Acts where God showed me who Tabitha was:

Now in Joppa there was a disciple named Tabitha (which translated in Greek is called Dorcas); this woman was abounding with deeds of kindness and charity which she continually did.

—Acts 9:36

. . . And all the widows stood beside him, weeping and showing all the tunics and garments that Dorcas used to make while she was with them.

—Acts 9:39

When God gave me the vision for this book, I asked Him if I could write the truth but in another name because I desired to protect the innocent. Immediately, the name Tabitha jumped into my mind.

Later, I perceived the word "lavender" should be my surname. I did not understand the reason for "lavender." I thought perhaps because it was going to be my color for this season of my life (and it used to be my favorite color). I discovered the root of the word "lavender" is the Latin word lavare, which means "to wash." The herb lavender probably received its name because it was often used in the purification of the body and the spirit. Research has found that lavender (the herb) soothes and calms.

So, my new name, Tabitha Lavender, is tied to my mission, as Paul's was tied to his mission. God has called me to abound in deeds of kindness and charity with women and to help sooth and calm.

> *What shall we say then? Are we to continue in sin so that grace may increase? May it never be! How shall we who died to sin still live in it? Or do you not know that all of us who have been baptized into Christ Jesus have been baptized into His death? Therefore we have been buried with Him through baptism into death, so that as Christ was raised from the dead through the glory of the Father, so we too might walk in newness of life.*
>
> —Romans 6:1–4

I pray that this book will help you on your journey to healing and to walking in the newness of Christ.

End Notes

1. Abortion Risks: A List of Major Psychological Complications Related to Abortion (2011). Retrieved July 16, 2016, from www.afterabortion.org

2. Cohen, Susan, 2013, Still True: Abortion Does Not Increase Women's Risk of Mental Health Problems, *Guttmacher Policy Review,* 16, 2, 13-22

3. Human Life Alliance (2010). www.humanlife.org. Did You Know? Advertising Supplement, 1-12

4. Howard, Dennis (2016). The Abortion Index. Retrieved November 8, 2016 from www.movementforabetteramerica.org.

5. Progressive Sanctification (2002-2017). Retrieved July 13, 2017 from www.AllAboutFollowingJesus.org.

6. Rankin, W. Duncan (2010). Being and Becoming. Retrieved from www.ligonier.org.

Resources

21 Day Brain Detox

http://21daybraindetox.com/

An online program designed by Dr. Caroline Leaf, neuroscientist and author of Switch on Your Brain: The Key to Peak Happiness, Thinking, and Health.

Bible Study Tools

biblestudytools.com

BibleStudyTools.com is the largest free online Bible website for verse search and in-depth studies. Search verses using the translation and version you like with over 29 to choose from.

Binding Up the Brokenhearted Bible Study

Healinghearts.org

With the support of a compassionate Healing Hearts Certified Counselor (online or in person if there is a group in your area), this study walks you through discovering how God's Word offers hope and healing from a past abortion.

David Guzik's Bible Commentary

enduringword.com

Enduring Word exists to promote the work of Christian discipleship and evangelism worldwide, mainly through the publication and dissemination of the Bible teaching work of David Guzik and likeminded people.

Human Life Alliance

Humanlife.org

Human Life Alliance promotes awareness of the inherent dignity and personhood of human life, born and preborn, without exception or compromise. Human Life Alliance proclaims and defends a culture of life and chastity through education, social and political awareness, and life-affirming alternatives to abortion, infanticide, assisted suicide, and euthanasia. Human Life Alliance accomplishes its mission in a spirit of prayer and non-violence.

How to Be Free from Bitterness

http://ccmbooks.org/bookstore/how-to-be-free-from-bitterness-booklet/

This is a Christian booklet of various essays written to help a person remove bitterness from their life.

Matrix Lifecare Center (formerly Lifecare)

Matrixcares.org

Matrix Lifecare Center is a pregnancy resource center in Lafayette/West Lafayette, Indiana, that provides caring support to women and men faced with difficult pregnancy decisions. Other services are also offered.

The Peacemaker: A Biblical Guide to Resolving Personal Conflict

Author: Ken Sande

In The Peacemaker, Ken Sande presents a comprehensive and practical theology for conflict resolution designed to bring about not only a cease-fire but also unity and harmony.

The Power of a Praying Woman

Author: Stormie Omartian

In The Power of a Praying Woman, you'll find personal illustrations, carefully selected Scriptures, and heartfelt prayers to help you trust God with deep longings, not just pressing needs. It covers every area of life with prayer to help you maintain a right heart before God.

Precepts Ministries International: The Inductive Bible Study People

Precept.org

Precepts is an organization that creates and sells Bible studies in various formats including Precept Upon Precept, In & Out, the New Inductive Study Series, the "Lord" Study Series, 40-Minute Study Series, and Discover 4 Yourself Inductive Bible Studies for Kids.

Still Waters

Stillwaters.org

Still Waters is a Christian retreat house that values the timeless need for silence, solitude, and spiritual companionship in order to better hear God's voice to be transformed by Him.

White Horse Christian Center

www.whcc.net

White Horse Christian Center is a revival celebration center promoting unity through diversity by growing a strong, healthy church family and equipping the body of Christ to do the work of the ministry. The church's motto: "Reaching others with the love of Christ."

Acknowledgments

This book would not have been written if it were not for God—Father, Son, and Holy Spirit. For Him, I am forever thankful. Chandler Bolt's Self Publishing School (self-publishingschool.com) was the tool that moved me from God's vision to putting words on the paper. I am also grateful for the love, support, and understanding that my husband, adult children, and daughter-in-love provided that gave me the time, space, and peace to write. I am grateful to my Bible study sisters and my Praying sisters in Christ. Your fellowship and encouragement is priceless. I would also like to thank my accountability partner from Self Publishing School, Charlene Kugler. Our theological discussions were enlightening and inspiring.

About the Author

Tabitha Lavender is an educator and author who has loved writing and learning since she was a little girl when she would fill diaries with her words and stick drawings. Her thirst for learning carried over into her Christian life. She has completed over 7 Precept Inductive Bible Studies and has facilitated numerous Bible Studies.

Ms. Lavender heart's desire is that people experience the love of Jesus Christ, and any way that she can be a part of that experience she is willing to allow the Lord to use her.

Ms. Lavender holds a Bachelor of Arts in Psychology and a Master of Arts in Clinical Psychology.